I0078890

THAT STAR-SPANGLED BANNER

The War, the Flag, and the National Anthem

by

Gabrielle Stewart

Illustrated by
John McNees

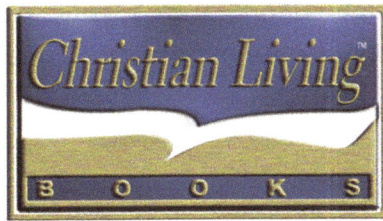

Christian Living™

B O O K S

Chapter 1 *O SAY CAN YOU SEE*

2014 was the 200th anniversary of our nation's national anthem. So this is a great year to research and write about it. In addition, as a native Marylander, it makes me proud to know what an important role the state of Maryland played in our national history.

"Maryland saved the nation in 1814 at the Battle of Baltimore, and this year Maryland will lead the nation in celebrating the bicentennial of the writing of the national anthem. The War of 1812 and the Star-Spangled Banner were pivotal in shaping our national identity and thread the tapestry of liberty for our nation," said the Governor of Maryland.

The state of Maryland led quite a celebration. Events featured re-enactments, fireworks, parades, and a maritime festival. I loved when 7,000 students from every county in Maryland joined together to make a living, 15-star, 15-stripe flag.

I visited the Smithsonian National Museum of American History, the Maryland Historical Society and Fort McHenry National Monument and Historic Shrine to prepare for this book. There are also lots of books and websites dedicated to that Star-Spangled Banner and the national anthem. However, I wanted to see these artifacts myself. What I learned and saw was very inspiring.

Chapter 2 *WHOSE BROAD STRIPES AND BRIGHT STARS*

According to a popular legend, the very first American flag was made by Betsy Ross, a Philadelphia seamstress. She was acquainted with George Washington, leader of the Continental Army, and other Philadelphians. The colors of the flag mean a lot to our country. White stands for purity and innocence. Red stands for hardiness and valor. Blue, the color of the Chief, stands for vigilance, perseverance, and justice.

Who made the flag for Fort McHenry? Some people think it was one woman, Mary Young Pickersgill, a local flag maker who was a widow. Actually, it was really Mary, her daughter, her two nieces, and an indentured African-American servant. Their names were Caroline, Eliza and Margaret Young, and Grace Wisher.

Lieutenant Colonel George Armistead was the commander of Fort McHenry. In 1813, he commissioned Mary Pickersgill to make the flag that would become "The Star-Spangled Banner." According to Elaine Landau, he said, "It is my desire to have a flag so large that the British will have no difficulty seeing it from a distance."

Pickersgill actually sent two flags to Fort McHenry: the huge flag and a smaller one they could use during stormy weather. Mary and her helpers were paid $405.90 for the two flags. Back then that was like $5,000—more than most people in Baltimore would earn in a year! It took the group six weeks to finish making the flags.

The huge, thirty-by-forty-two-foot flag was too big for the small rooms of Mary's house. So she moved her work across the street to Claggett's Brewery. At the brewery, they put the pieces of the flag together and placed fifteen cotton stars on the blue cotton. Today we have fifty stars on our flag. Each star represents one of the fifty states. Back then we only had fifteen stars on the flag because we didn't have as many states.

The Armistead family owned the flag. The flag was thirty by forty-two feet in the summer of 1813. However, the Armistead family gave snippets of the flag away as souvenirs and gifts over the years. In fact, one of the fifteen stars was cut out and given away in the 1800s. Where that star is now, no one knows.

The flag was in the hands of the Armistead family until it was given to the Smithsonian Institute in 1907. By the time the museum got the flag, it was missing a star and was eight feet shorter because of the Armistead family's generous snippet gifts. The flag is now at the National Museum of American History.

Chapter 3 THE ROCKET'S RED GLARE

Most Americans know of the Revolutionary War. It began in 1775 as the American colonies went to war with Great Britain to gain their freedom. The peace treaty was finally signed in 1783 and the United States of America was born. The War of 1812 is not as famous as the Revolutionary War. Still, many remember the War of 1812 as the "second war of independence." It ushered in a new sense of national unity and pride. It brought several generals to the forefront including Andrew Jackson, Winfield Scott and Jacob Brown. No less than four men rose to prominence and ultimately to the presidency: Andrew Jackson, John Quincy Adams, James Monroe and William Henry Harrison.

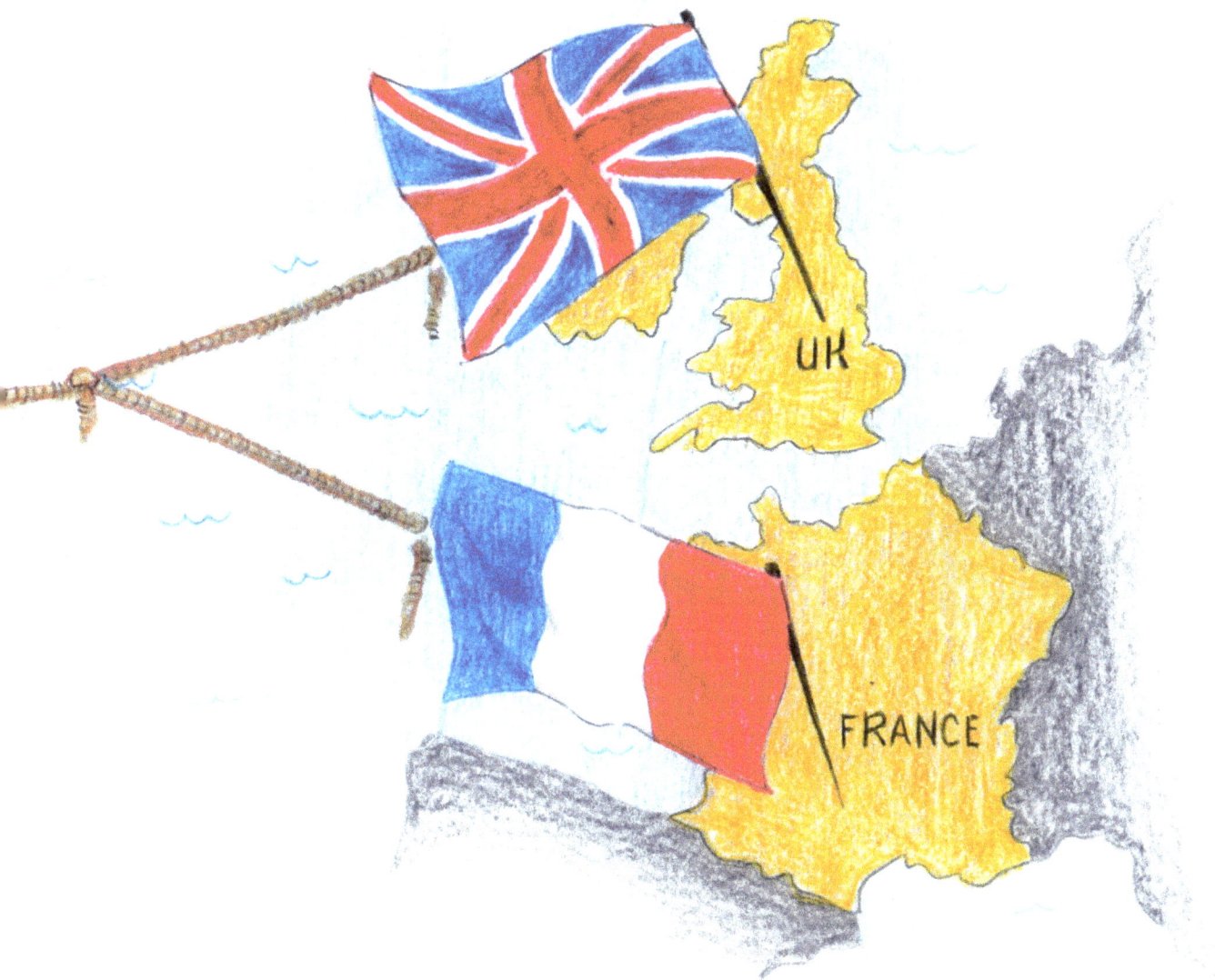

George Washington, the first US president, warned Americans about getting into other nations' disagreements. However, when Great Britain went to war against France and their new leader, Napoleon, the British and the French made it very difficult to stay out of the conflict.

Young America enjoyed trade with both countries. Wanting to cut off supplies en route to the enemy, each side tried to block the US from trading with the other. So, Great Britain forced ships that traded with France to pay fees. France ordered all ships not to stop at any British ports. So America was in an awful position. In addition to this, Great Britain began an unfair practice called impressment in which the British would capture US ships and force American sailors to work on the British ships.

In 1807, US President Thomas Jefferson supported the Embargo Act which stopped trade between the United States and other countries. However, this really hurt American businesses. This continued until 1810 when Congress ended the Embargo Act. However, the United States decided to choose between the two countries, Great Britain and France. Because Napoleon pretended he would cooperate, the United States chose to deal with France and not with Great Britain. Ultimately, war seemed like the only option to the new US president, James Madison. On June 18, 1812, the US Congress declared war on Great Britain.

At that time, Great Britain was a far more powerful nation with the world's greatest navy. The United States had very little money, a small army, a small navy, and only a few trained officers. To make matters worse, New England, the richest section of the United States, refused to help and didn't send any money or soldiers.

Great Britain's forces were divided between the US war and the ongoing war with France. As the war went on, both Great Britain and the United States won some battles and lost others. In 1814, the British invaded Washington DC and set fire to the Capitol, the White House, the Treasury Building, and the Library of Congress. Then the troops headed to Baltimore.

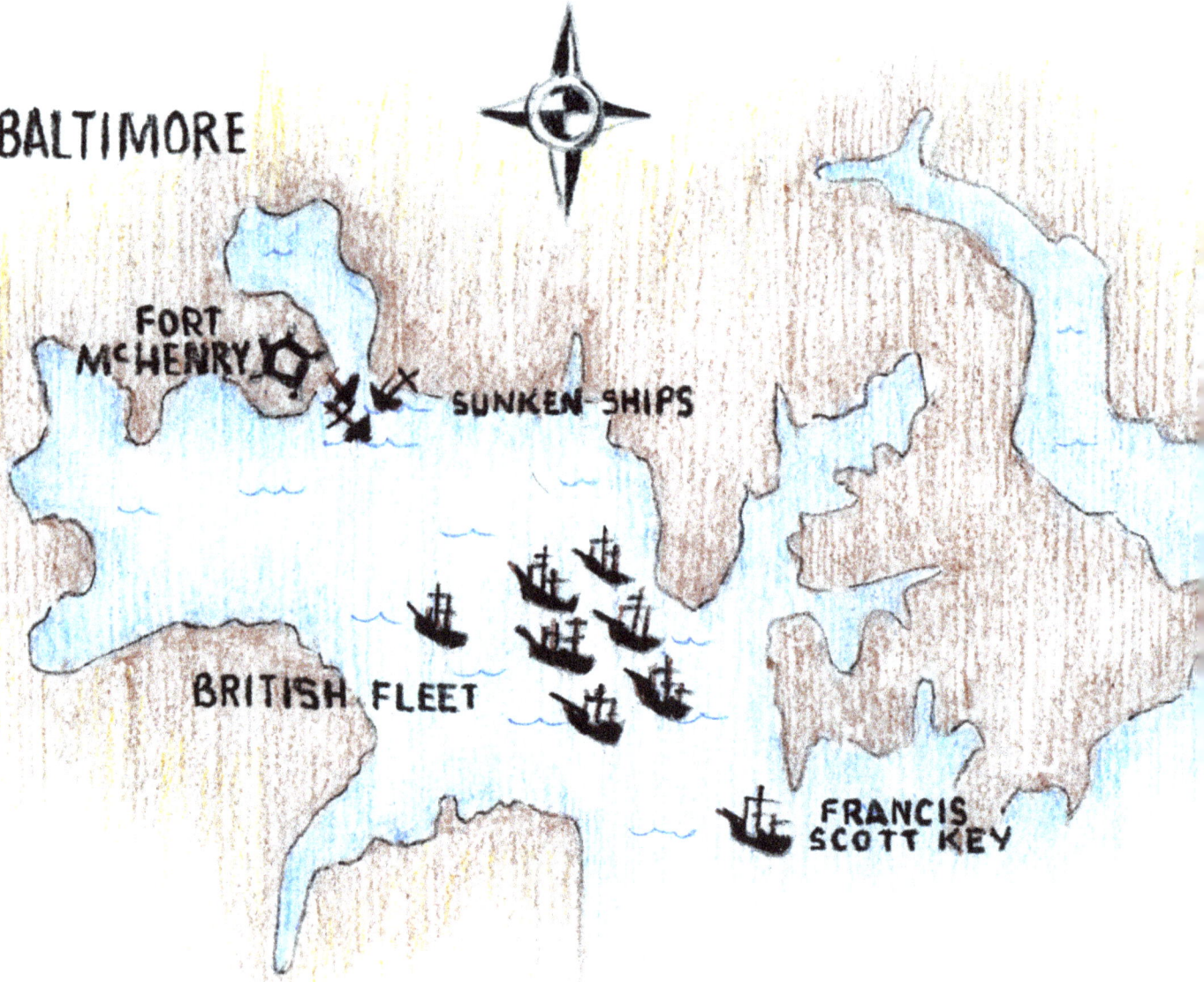

BALTIMORE

FORT McHENRY

SUNKEN SHIPS

BRITISH FLEET

FRANCIS SCOTT KEY

US General Samuel Smith led citizens to pull together and dig trenches for cannon guns. He also told ship owners to sink their ships in the Baltimore harbor. The British ships were not able to enter the port of Baltimore because it was blocked by the sunken ships.

Fort McHenry guarded the Baltimore harbor. A giant American flag few above the five-sided fort. When the British arrived, an American truce ship was in the harbor. That ship was where talks with the British took place. An American lawyer, Francis Scott Key, was on that ship. As he was a prominent attorney, US officials had asked Key to secure the release of physician, Dr. William Beanes, who had been taken prisoner by the British.

British ships, unable to enter the harbor, fired on the fort for twenty-five hours. US soldiers fought back. Key watched the whole battle from the truce ship.

14

Chapter 4 *THAT STAR-SPANGLED BANNER*

When Francis Scott Key woke up the next morning and saw the America flag still waving, he marveled that the flag had survived the ferocious British bombing. It inspired him to write what became our national anthem.

It was not always a song. Francis Scott Key actually wrote a poem made up of four paragraphs. He started writing the poem "Defence of Fort McHenry" on the back of a letter. Only one-fourth of that poem, the first paragraph, became our national anthem.

Have you ever thought about what the words really mean? *O say can you see, by the dawn's early light.* After a very long evening filled with bombs and fighting, Francis Scott Key woke up very early the next morning. What did he see? *What so proudly we hail'd at the twilight's last gleaming?* Francis Scott Key caught a glimpse of the flag the night of the battle, just before he went to sleep. He saluted it for what he thought was one last time.

Whose broad stripes and bright stars through the perilous fight. He saw the US flag the night before when he saluted it before going to bed. *O'er the ramparts we watch'd were so gallantly streaming? And the rocket's red glare, the bombs bursting in air. Gave proof through the night that our flag was still there, O say does that star-spangled banner yet wave.* The last time Key saw it, the flag was waving majestically over the fort. He caught glimpses of it in the dark, when the bombs were exploding.

O'er the land of the free and the home of the brave? Key was surprised that the flag survived. People might underestimate the inspiration of the flag. But when you take the time to think about it, you see the true meaning of the poem. Where can you see the original poem? Its permanent home is at the Maryland Historical Society in Baltimore.

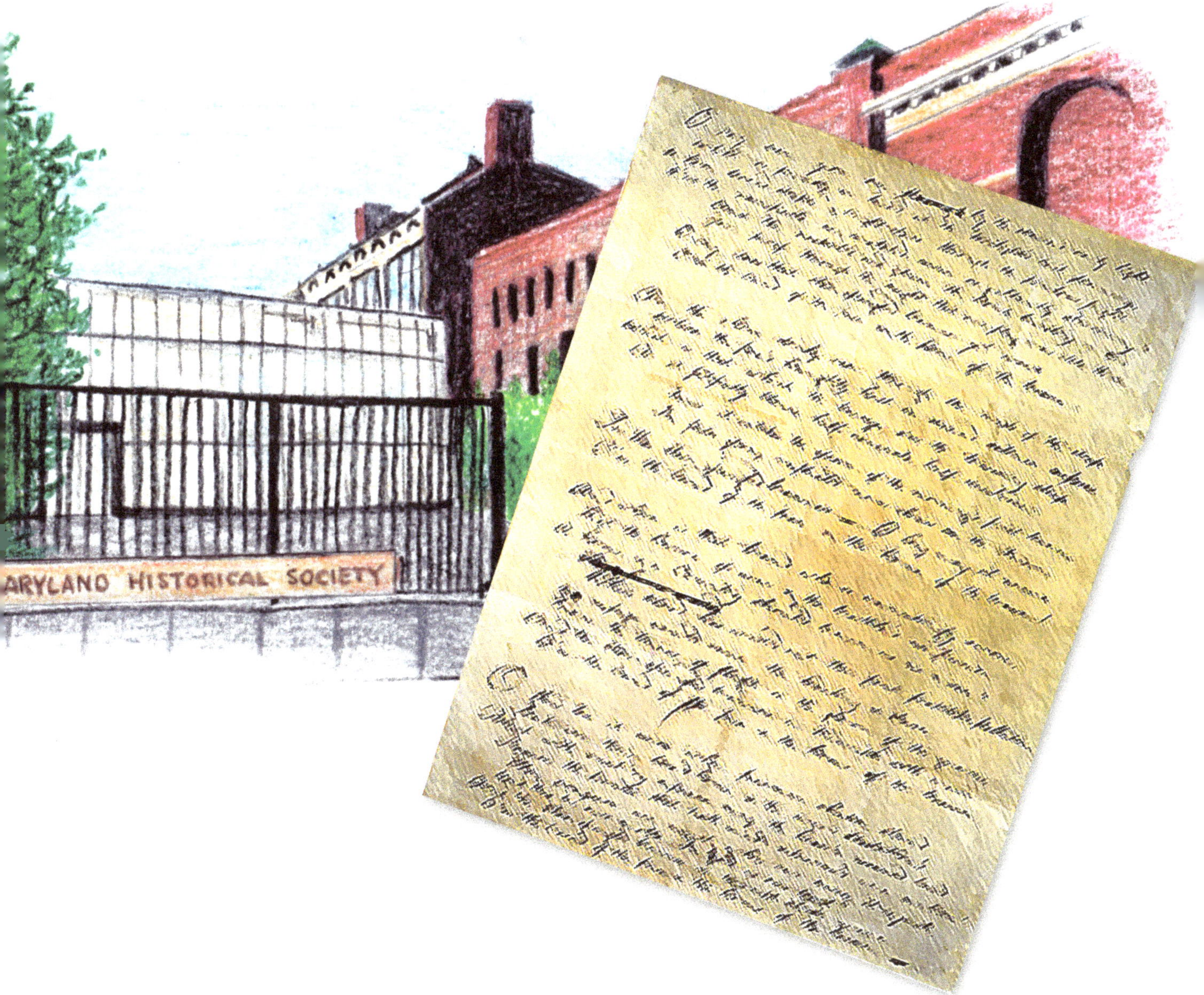
ARYLAND HISTORICAL SOCIETY

Defence of Fort McHenry

by Francis Scott Key

O say can you see, by the dawn's early light,

What so proudly we hail'd at the twilight's last gleaming,

Whose broad stripes and bright stars through the perilous fight

O'er the ramparts we watch'd were so gallantly streaming?

And the rocket's red glare, the bombs bursting in air,

Gave proof through the night that our flag was still there,

O say does that star-spangled banner yet wave

O'er the land of the free and the home of the brave?

On the shore dimly seen through the mists of the deep

Where the foe's haughty host in dread silence reposes,

What is that which the breeze, o'er the towering steep,

As it fitfully blows, half conceals, half discloses?

Now it catches the gleam of the morning's first beam,

In full glory reflected now shines in the stream,

'Tis the star-spangled banner - O long may it wave

O'er the land of the free and the home of the brave!

And where is that band who so vauntingly swore,

That the havoc of war and the battle's confusion

A home and a Country should leave us no more?

Their blood has wash'd out their foul footstep's pollution.

No refuge could save the hireling and slave

From the terror of flight or the gloom of the grave,

And the star-spangled banner in triumph doth wave

O'er the land of the free and the home of the brave.

O thus be it ever when freemen shall stand

Between their lov'd home and the war's desolation!

Blest with vict'ry and peace may the heav'n rescued land

Praise the power that hath made and preserv'd us a nation!

Then conquer we must, when our cause it is just,

And this be our motto - "In God is our trust,"

And the star-spangled banner in triumph shall wave

O'er the land of the free and the home of the brave.

BALTIMORE PATRIOT

AND
EVENING ADVERTISER.

Tuesday Evening, Sept. 20.

BY MUNROE & FRENCH,
NO. 54, SOUTH-STREET, BALTIMORE.

DAILY Paper, *eight dollars a year.*—COUN-
TRY (three times a week) *five.*
☞ Advertisements appear in both papers.
☞ All letters addressed to the Editors must
be post paid.

THE PARTERRE.

Defence of Fort M'Henry.

[☞ The following beautiful and animating
effusion, which is destined long to outlast
the occasion, and outlive the impulse, which
produced it, has already been extensively
circulated. In our first renewal of publica-
tion, we rejoice in an opportunity to enliven
the sketch of an exploit so illustrious,
with strains which so richly celebrate it.]

ED. PAT.

The annexed song was composed under
the following circumstances—A gentleman
had left Baltimore, in a flag of truce for the
purpose of getting released from the British
fleet a friend of his, who had been captured
at Malborough. He went as far as the mouth
of the Patuxent, and was not permitted to
return lest the intended attack on Baltimore
should be disclosed. He was therefore
brought up the bay to the mouth of the Pa-
tapsco, where the flag vessel was kept under
the guns of a frigate, and he was compelled
to witness the bombardment of Fort M'Henry, which the Admiral had boasted that he
would carry in a few hours, and that the city
must fall. He watched the flag at the Fort
through the whole day with an anxiety that
can be better felt than described, until the
night prevented him from seeing it. In the
night he watched the Bomb-Shells, and at
early dawn his eye was again greeted by the
proudly-waving flag of his country.

Tune—ANACREON IN HEAVEN.

O! say can you see, by the dawn's early light,
What so proudly we hail'd at the twilight's last gleaming,
Whose broad stripes and bright stars through
the perilous fight,
O'er the ramparts we watch'd, were so gallantly streaming?
And the rockets' red glare, the Bombs bursting in the night, that our Flag
was still there—
O! say does that star-spangled Banner yet wave,
O'er the land of the free, and the home
of the brave?

Chapter 5   LAND OF THE FREE AND THE HOME OF THE BRAVE

When Francis Scott Key finished writing the poem, he gave it to a relative. That relative had flyers printed up. Soon the inspirational poem was reproduced in newspapers all over the country.

The poem became a song which was first sung at a Baltimore theatre on October 19, 1914. In 1889, "The Star-Spangled Banner" became the US Navy's official song. In 1931, Congress made the song our national anthem. President Hoover made it official by signing a bill to make it so. So it took one hundred and sixteen years for Francis Scott Key's poem to become our national anthem.

I visited the Smithsonian's National Museum of American History. What an awesome place! That Star-Spangled Banner is there on display. No one is allowed to take pictures of it. According to the Smithsonian website: "It's our job as museum professionals to protect this precious object, and the greatest threat to the flag over the long term is light. The flag's fibers absorb the energy from light, which causes harmful chemical reactions and deterioration."

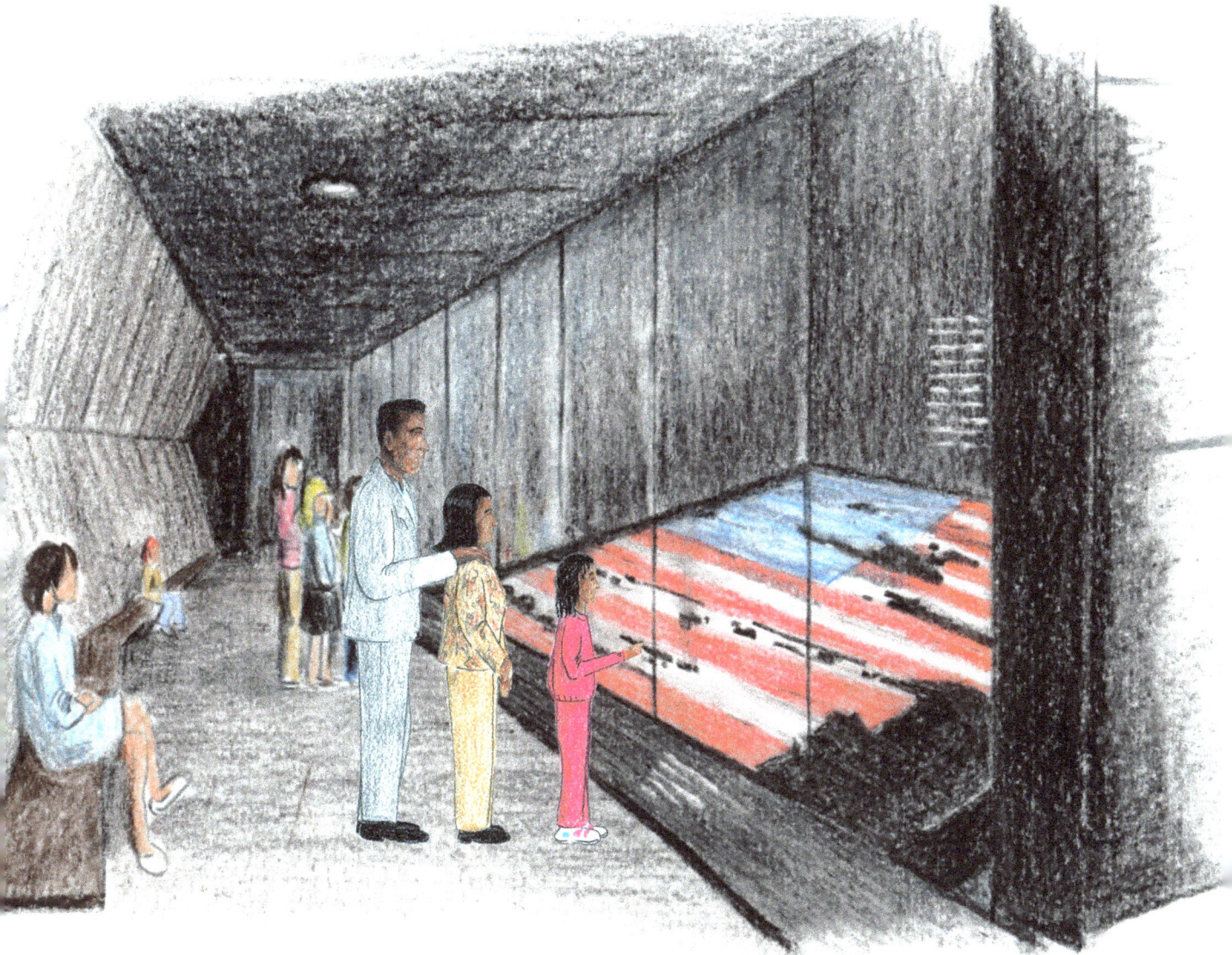

That flag is HUGE. Even though it is eight feet smaller than its original size, it is still awesome to see. It takes your breath away. People were constantly coming in to view its beauty. Some people just took a seat, right in front of it, and stared for long periods of time. The museum had cool interactive displays that gave interesting facts about the flag, the war, and the national anthem. I had a lot of fun going through all of it.

I've heard many different versions of the national anthem. My mother's favorite is by Whitney Houston, sung at the 1991 Super Bowl. There is a picture of Whitney Houston singing the national anthem in the exhibit. So her version must be a favorite of many people. The national anthem always brings my mother to tears. It wasn't until I did the research for this book that I really understood why.

London 2012

GABRIELLE STEWART is ten-years-old. She's in 4th grade at a school for academically gifted students. This year, Gabby started the first ever student newsletter at her school. She serves as editor-in-chief and has recruited several department editors to work with her. Gabby loves spending time with her family and friends, math, reading, soccer, gymnastics, hand knitting, fashion design, glitter, glam and hot pink. She lives with her family in Mitchellville, Maryland.

Interact on ThatStarSpangledBanner.com

ACKNOWLEDGMENTS

To the Lord for all of His blessings. To my parents, Derwin and Kimberly Stewart, for always encouraging and inspiring me. To my wonderful grandparents, Irma Hinton, Christine Stewart and Shellie Stewart, for loving me, unconditionally. To my Grandpa in Heaven, the great Chuck Hinton, whose book I read whenever I miss him. To my fabulous Aunties and all my family and friends for their support. To my best friends for being awesome. To Mr. Etheredge, my Social Studies teacher, for making this subject so much fun. I love and appreciate you all.

–Gabby

Founding Members of
That Star-Spangled Banner Appreciation Club

Dean & Bonnie Baker	Abigail Gross	Courtney Lipscomb
Shawn & Sheryl Brown	Susan Hay	Meryll Paclarin
Greg Caudle	Eleanor Hinton	Lance & Brenda MacNiven
Trina Collier	Irma Hinton	Dimas, Tiffany, Dallas & Skylar
Marcus Davis	Clark & Edith Jones	Christine Stewart
Nate & Paulette Davis	Obadiah Kegege	Derwin & Kimberly Stewart
Rico & Tonja Durant	Christy Lipscomb	Shellie Stewart

Text copyright © 2015 by Gabrielle Stewart

Illustrations copyright © 2015 by John McNees

All rights reserved, including the right of reproduction in whole or in part in any form.

Hardback ISBN 9781562290037
Paperback ISBN 9781562290658
eBook ISBN 9781562290665
Audiobook ISBN 9781562290672

Christian Living Books, Inc.
P. O. Box 7584
Largo, MD 20792
www.ChristianLivingBooks.com

Special discounts are available for bulk purchases of this book.
Please contact Special Sales at info@christianlivingbooks.com.

Printed in the United States of America.

Library of Congress Cataloging-in-Publication Data

Stewart, Gabrielle, 2004-
  That star-spangled banner : the war, the flag, and the national anthem / by Gabrielle Stewart ; illustrated by John McNees.
     pages cm
  Audience: Grades 4-6.
  ISBN 978-1-56229-033-7 (hardback : alk. paper) -- ISBN 978-1-56229-065-8 (pbk.) -- ISBN 978-1-56229-066-5 (ebook) -- ISBN 978-1-56229-067-2 (audiobook) 1. Baltimore, Battle of, Baltimore, Md., 1814--Juvenile literature. 2. United States--History--War of 1812--Flags--Juvenile literature. 3. Flags--United States--History--19th century--Juvenile literature. 4. Key, Francis Scott, 1779-1843--Juvenile literature. 5. Star-spangled banner (Song)--Juvenile literature. I. McNees, John, illustrator. II. Title.

  E356.B2S88 2015
  973.5'2--dc23

                    2015011976

.

www.ingramcontent.com/pod-product-compliance
Lightning Source LLC
Chambersburg PA
CBHW081342090426

42737CB00017B/3253